One Soul's Journey- a Mystic's Way Home.

Josie Hopkins

BALBOA
PRESS

A DIVISION OF HAY HOUSE

ISBN: 978-1-4525-6318-3 (sc)
ISBN: 978-1-4525-6320-6 (hc)
ISBN: 978-1-4525-6319-0 (e)

Library of Congress Control Number: 2012921402

Balboa Press books may be ordered through booksellers or by contacting:
Balboa Press
A Division of Hay House
1663 Liberty Drive
Bloomington, IN 47403
www.balboapress.com
1-(877) 407-4847

Because of the dynamic nature of the Internet, any web addresses or links contained in
this book may have changed since publication and may no longer be valid. The views
expressed in this work are solely those of the author and do not necessarily reflect the
views of the publisher, and the publisher hereby disclaims any responsibility for them.

The author of this book does not dispense medical advice or prescribe the use
of any technique as a form of treatment for physical, emotional, or medical
problems without the advice of a physician, either directly or indirectly. The
intent of the author is only to offer information of a general nature to help you
in your quest for emotional and spiritual well-being. In the event you use any
of the information in this book for yourself, which is your constitutional right,
the author and the publisher assume no responsibility for your actions.

Any people depicted in stock imagery provided by Thinkstock are models,
and such images are being used for illustrative purposes only.
Certain stock imagery © Thinkstock.

Printed in the United States of America

Balboa Press rev. date: 11/12/2012

Angelic Chorus

There is an angelic chorus being brought
to us right now, can you hear it?

Can you hear it coming from the rays of sunset that
beam out to you through the trees — reaching to find you
with the sacred symbols that carry the tones? Can you
recognize the angels' chorus as they weave it into the birds'
conversations as they speak to each other, combining the
different songs to form their sacred array of tones?

Can you sense the holiness as you get a glimpse of these
tones? Really listen and you will hear and you will
also feel. For it is the holiness inside that causes you
to recognize the chorus without. Honor it — know it —
and you will realize that you have always been a part
of that Angelic Chorus. It has been there forever.

Gratitudes

There is a deep place of gratitude in my heart for the scaffolding that Black Elk lovingly provided, awakening my soul to take the sacred journey back home. I am so very grateful.

In reflecting on the past seven months of writing this book, I am filled with a gratefulness beyond anything I could possibly describe for Teresa of Avila. Her ever continuing guidance was the most intimate and deepest of experiences, and her visitations brought her sacred wisdom, filling me with such profound love for her. I have been very blessed for her guidance to write this book, and in all areas of my life. Thank you, Teresa.

Gratitude for Lynn Keasler, who had the amazing ability to decipher my handwriting, enabling her to type this manuscript. And whose dedication to the Divine is opening her to become the radiant flower that she was meant to be.

Contents

Introduction

As we progress through each lifetime,
our soul's journey
could be thought of as a snowflake.

As a snowflake, each soul is unique, and yet all are created through the same mysterious process. Through this process of becoming matter, each individual snowflake forms its own pattern, its own energetic structure. There are many snowflake patterns that are very simple with only the extending of a few branches to create their shape. Others come with a further layer upon the simple structure, and still others create many layers of complex and intricate levels before coming down to earth. The mystery of how snowflakes are actually created still eludes us today. Because it is a mysterious journey, they hold an element of wonderment to those who care to observe them. There is a Grace that seems to embody them as they silently descend down to us. The feeling that makes us smile as we watch them is Grace. We are simply connecting, in that brief moment, with what is within us to what is without.

The journey of our soul, our essence, is so strikingly similar. If we were to sit above earth for a moment, above time as we know it at the earthly level, we would see how quickly our stay in this lifetime is, just as the snowflake so rapidly melts after being created. It possibly would enable us to glean a purpose for our soul being here with a better understanding of the brief span at which we are given to open and live that purpose. When we have multiple layers formed in our life's purpose, as the many layered snowflake, we are given the opportunity through the Universe to experience a multitude of situations in order that our simple branches can extend out to the more intricate patterns held within our design. It is not that these souls are special or better than the simpler designed souls, they only, through lifetimes of added patterns, are created now to become highly defined in their formations.

When we are called as a Mystic into our soul's purpose, we are asked to push our branches of ice formations, so to speak, to the farthest limits, thereby creating the most exquisite form possible. It means transcending – moving past – dissolving all cultural, religious, and ancestral beliefs, to truly know the Divine. It means finding the sacred in ourselves and in every part of our lives. In order to accomplish this, our journey through life is filled with many challenges, all for the purpose of evolving into the one single destination of our soul… to reconnect with the mystery, the Divine Creator. We must learn to embody Grace, as the snowflake, to unfold our descent into wonderment, and to then give our Grace out to all others.

Many have lived the path of the Mystic, those known and unknown. They have all brought their wisdom onto this planet, enabling us to nurture our souls with a glimpse of understanding from their experiences. We have been truly blessed with the deep and rich revelations from those such as Teresa of Avila, a 16th century Carmelite Nun. Her strength and faith elevated her far beyond her religion and fear. Her dedication to her inner life was absolutely amazing as she came to know the Divine through experiences that could have cost her life during the bleak and dark period of the Inquisition. Because of her love and conviction to the Divine, she spoke truth when no other women dared to, enabling her to become one of the greatest Mystics ever known.

As more of us have come to realize, at this now crucial time in humanity, the Divine truths, and the understanding of the mystical laws that lie deep in our souls needs to be allowed to come alive. As many already have realized, it *must* come alive for survival. But we have to know how to access the truth. Only by taking the journey deep into ourselves may we find the truth. It is the path of straightforwardness to the Divine, beyond *any* religion or culture. All the great Mystics knew that at the core of our nature lies a Divine way of loving, and that it takes determination to find that way of loving. Many humans have accessed the wisdom of this core, for wisdom comes from experience. They have emerged and *are* emerging to share their part of the dance in the Universe. And from that, many have been guided towards their way home.

I, too, wish to contribute as an individual, another personal expression of that dance. We are all here to help each other. *"Experience is not what happens, but what we do with what happens."* – *(Aldous Huxley)*

My intention for sharing my journey, in the most honest and open way that I possibly can, is to tenderly help awaken those glimpsing the stirrings felt from inside their inner self. And also to humbly offer guidance from the process of my unfolding, to those who are experiencing things in their lives that are causing them to question what is happening. As we further proceed into this time of the Mystics and all of humanity on their unique paths being called to action, I feel there is the need to have an honest sharing, in a heartfelt manner, for a way in which to navigate back through the rigorous journey into the interior of oneself. This journey that I so lovingly share might seem unusual because the transformation process that took place for me was without teachers on the physical plane. What is offered is an authentic unfolding into the powerful and sacred place that lies within all of us and the tools needed along the way for the growth necessary for that unfolding process. The revelations to deeper levels of consciousness came through my soul with the assistance of Higher Beings, thus allowing access to the ancient wisdom which, through time, came to be revealed to me as the calling of a Mystic.

A Mystic is someone who is called to know the mystery of the Divine through experiencing challenging situations that cause their soul to expand the branches of its snowflake. Someone who, when called, becomes devoted with their love for the Divine taking them deeper and deeper into the mystery, training themselves, through their devotion, to truly know the interconnectedness of all beings. And then putting this knowing into an everyday practice. Someone who wants to live a pure-souled life. They do not choose this calling, they are chosen to this calling and their soul is set on the path of service for assisting others. They learn through their experiences how to bring their wisdom to humanity. The many stages of progressing through this journey are what I humbly offer. It is important to understand the sacred stages which we all pass through on our spiritual journeys, for the more we are aware of how these stages flow... the awakening, the purification, the battle with the ego in the dark night of the soul, and finally the resurrection of our soul lit with Divine light... the easier it will be to progress through these phases. The intensity with which we are asked to experience them depends on our own path for our soul's evolution. Each soul knows what it needs to experience, and the appropriate lessons are always being brought to it, no matter which spiritual path we are experiencing.

*By progressing through our Mystical journey
we allow our individual pattern of exquisite beauty
to carry the Grace from our unique snowflake
out into the world.*

Chapter 1

Beginning the Journey

I N MY LIFETIME, THE JOURNEY began early, dying in a car accident at the age of 6 years old. As a consequence of this trauma, I spent many months throughout my childhood in isolation. Because my body was propelled through the windshield, half of my face was lost, therefore bandages encasing my entire head as a mummy were necessary. This process took place after each surgery for the next seven years. Instead of moving out "into" the world, I was pulled back into the solitude of the soul, thereby reversing the "normal" childhood process. In these quiet places, experiences of brilliant purple colors, movement and images from the third eye were fascinating, deep and real.

Because of the many surgeries, the time spent in isolation gave me the opportunity to reside in the inner self. This enabled me to truly know myself. I find it almost amusing now to reflect on the symbolic reason of why I was so in love with the "I Dream of Jeannie" show when I was young. I would eagerly watch and even made myself a beautiful bottle with eyes on it, "pretending" to put myself into it. The whole concept of going "within your bottle" to be in your home, and finding your wisdom, and then being summoned out to be of service to others, truly resonated with me. My soul was my "learning world" instead of the earthly world. I was not aware that I was viewing the world in a different way than other children. All I knew was that there was a difficulty feeling compatible when interacting with others because I didn't see the world the same way they did.

As with all children who are not accepted, the pain of rejection became my challenge. As we all know, children can be and in fact have always been very cruel. Name calling and ridiculing cuts like a knife. However, it is a two-edged sword. The pain experienced through those difficult situations also holds the potential to allow the child to transcend the pain on some levels, because it almost forces them to "rise above it," and to find their individualism early on. Many times, children who have gone through severe illness or disfigurement reach a level of surrender and acceptance that keeps them connected with their true essence. These children have a simplicity and strength that other children never had the chance to access. They shine this simplicity throughout their lives, and they often seem very mature for their age. Their soul has brought them wisdom that the "normal" child missed by being out in the world as society knows it. This perfectly designed journey through childhood forms a beautiful branch on their snowflake.

Growing up Catholic raised many questions for me. I witnessed the hypocrisy of people in church, and it disturbed me that even though we were all being taught to "love thy neighbor as thyself," people were pushing to get out of the church doors and parking lot first, while at the same time pretending they weren't actually doing what they were doing. I saw very clearly the dogma my parents and others held as their way of living. My soul knew that this simply was not the truth. I intuitively asked myself "Why are people living like that?" But I had to travel much farther on my journey before I could fully learn how to embrace the truth, and put it into an active service for others.

As a teen, I reached for the illusions of the ego as life continued with challenges. Alcoholism with my Mom, and date rape, were a few of the issues to be dealt with. I was insecure and feared that no one would want to marry me and help raise a family. All that felt right in me was raising a family. The desire to build and take care of a home, one so different from my parent's home, had been a strong desire even in my teens. The word "home" had an inner importance that I was not aware of at the time. I only knew that home for "us" would have a simple freedom that many families didn't have. The strong intent to share the wonderment of nature and the innocence of playtime with "our" young children was something I longed for.

It always makes me smile to look back and realize how the Divine brings just the right person into our lives at just the right time. I was truly blessed with a life companion. He lived very much in society's ways, but shining out was his authentic self that held the same values of simple family life. He was compassionate and patient, and I knew I would learn patience just by being with him. In some inherent way we both knew that the meeting of our souls fit the cosmic puzzle pieces needed for this life together. Shortly after our first child was born, my soul began "tapping me on the shoulder," as they say. A deep knowing surfaced from within. I knew with all my being that living a simple rural life on a small farm was a necessity for myself and my growing family. I was almost 21 at the time, and for the next 9 years, even though we still lived in town with five small children, the determination for the farm never wavered. I taught myself how to live a simple rural life. I learned how to tend animals, cook on a wood cook stove, and chop wood, among other things.

There were many glimpses of awareness and insights. One situation in particular brought a deep awareness to me. One of our neighbors who was about my age, (late 20's at the time), was upset about something she thought was important that was taking place somewhere in the world. I don't remember the details, but I do remember telling her that I was not familiar with what she was talking about. At that point she told me that "I was just a simpleton." I went home and cried. While I was crying, I recall a part of me feeling degraded and somewhat ignorant. While at the same time another part of me felt a peace about being a simpleton. Of course I didn't know then that while the ego was feeling diminished, my soul was speaking to me of humble peace. It felt familiar at the time, and I remember taking comfort in that peace. Yet, once again, I realized how strange it sometimes was interacting with others. At that time it was the feeling of "not fitting in," as so many of us seem to experience at this point in our journey. We know we are meant to be interacting, but do not really understand how to.

All through this I was finding a deeper sense of self. And the innocent child within found delights and joys in all of our children that I never dreamed possible. I was not, however, aware of the ego's ways and the how it grants us the go ahead to continually ask in prayer for what we want. The light bulb that had been turned on allowed the knowing of how to be closer to the Divine through nature and simplicity, but it had not been turned up to maximum brightness. I used what we would call "Prayer 101," those beginning prayers we say that contain the expectations and agendas for our lives that reflect our level of consciousness.

This level of prayer reaches to the Divine with the underlying, and not recognized, ways of asking to be given exactly what we want, when we want it. Our prayers are also seeking to keep everyone that we love safe. We truly believe, through our rational mind, with which we are doing the praying, that this is the way of prayer. We do not realize we are ultimately trying to control the "safety factor" in our lives through asking the Divine to serve *us* and what *we* need. The underlying fear of change and loss keeps us from seeing anything beyond this way of praying. This level of consciousness continues until our soul starts to teach us the truth of how to humbly pray.

Chapter 2

The Spiritual Death and
the Unfolding Soul

THE CONCEPTS OF MOVING TO the farm and the determination of birthing our babies at home were not easily accepted by my husband or our families. Because my inner self knew the inner truths I had to honor, it taught me strength to stay in those truths no matter what others said. And it also taught me endurance. I have since come to realize that the Grace of Fortitude comes to those who have found the words "know thyself" to be an unfolding truth. The Grace of Fortitude, the ability to bear up to other judgments, gave me the stamina and courage to proceed with what worked for me. I had been blessed with that Grace.

After the passing of nine years, I found that the day we moved to the farm was like nothing I'd ever experienced before. There was a great joy as I stepped onto the land, and an incredible deep knowing took place. It cosmically reached down into my soul, and I knew in that moment I had a sacred contract to fulfill here. It felt as though it was something that would be revealed and unfold in time. And yet, at the same time, I intuitively knew I had lived on this land before. The feeling of home was so abundantly prevalent as we began to build our rural life by planting trees, gardens, and living with nature. There were many experiences of birth and death with our farm animals, and the children learned how to honor both. We were making it the homestead that I had passionately held within my heart.

As the years flew by, three more babies were born here and each day was filled. Through the busyness of children and chores, there was always a deeper knowing of another purpose for being on the farm. One evening, a few years later, that clear vision revealed itself in a micro-second. This download enabled me to see how to build the antique shop I had envisioned. It must have seemed like a farfetched idea to others, because at the time, I truly had no money, no time, and very little knowledge to start this type of business.

Through Divine inspiration I was shown that this was the next creative step to take here on this land. It appeared to everyone to be an unsafe endeavor which, I later learned, is precisely how Divine inspiration works! It was as if my soul was propelling me forward to make it a reality, therefore, there was no fear of failure or humiliation. In allowing the knowing from within to guide me to build and continually expand, the energy of the shop has always had only one real purpose, which has provided a space, a place where people could come and feel relaxed in nature, while finding the pieces of history, the antiques they were looking for. But more importantly, a place to feel that their soul could be nourished on whatever level they could feel it. It was not known to me at that time what else it would evolve into and what the Divine purpose was for building this space. Gradually, the beauty of the antiques filled the antique shop and our home. My husband and I so resonated with the old woods of handmade furniture, and being surrounded with everything "old" felt so right.

Because the world of business, (competition and the drive to make money), never entered into the endeavor, the energy that created this space has made it a success, but it was not my success, it was the Divine's. This is not to say that the journey with the antique business has been an easy one, but the passion to create what was being directed to me was the driving force that always propelled me on. It was at this time, that I felt as if I was being asked by the universe, the Divine, to expand the branches of the snowflake. As I continued in the busyness of daily life with eight growing children, I could feel something stirring inside me. I found myself with questions coming from somewhere within asking, *"Why am I really here?"* Moments of wondering, *"Why does this feel like there is something more?"* became prevalent.

Everything in my life started to feel like it was not answering those questions. The trickling of the Divine waters had started to penetrate into my consciousness, and at that point it felt as a pulling from inside. I felt as though I was looking for something and didn't know what it was. It was subtle, but never subsided. Not realizing what was in my energy field for growth, I stayed busy with daily life. My inner self felt as though it craved some direction for answering those questions and yet my mind told me I was too busy to stop and find out. It is crucial at these crossroad times to ponder on what is really happening, but I did not. As with all soul contracts, when Divine timing aligns with lessons needed to be learned, we are somehow stopped and taken out of our daily routine by something challenging that shakes our world.

That is what came into my life in November of 1999, a second accident. Because I was hit at 108 mph, I was confronted once again with facial surgery. The amount of facial injuries were not as extensive as the first accident, but the surgery had to be performed while I was awake. It was then, at that point, the Divine provided me with an opportunity that changed my life forever. Stepping through the most intense fear I'd ever known, a total surrender took place. I remember being strapped down to the operating table with fear becoming so overwhelming it felt like I could not bear it. At that point, I saw my life zipping past in front of me, and in that micro-second the love for the Divine became so much more intense than the fear. I allowed myself to die the spiritual death. It was then that I experienced feeling the incredible union with the deep peace that we call God, the Divine. I was watching my body being operated on and could hear the conversations between the doctor and nurse, as I resided in an abundantly sacred peace. This death allowed a shift in consciousness so profound that the sacred Divine space in my soul became accessed like never before. And yet, at the same time, this soul essence was a familiar place – it was home.

As I began to recover I found myself almost feeling lost. I continually cried releasing past hurts and dealing with the trauma. I started meditating… something I'd never consciously done as an adult, but quickly found, as in my childhood, it was a natural state of being. During these mediations, a Native American Shaman, a Lakota Holy Man named Black Elk, began teaching me his ways of living in a sacred manner. I did not know what a Shaman was, not being familiar with the Native American culture. At first I just found it strange, until I began to learn that I too was a Shaman, a wounded healer. I found that Black Elk was weaving into the very fabric of my existence the sacred teachings of all nature and the animal kingdom. I was being trained to learn the Shaman's ways of true wisdom. I started seeing everything in its sacred essence. Many times while observing the simplest of nature's works, I would be taken with its beauty and brought to tears, as an overwhelming gratitude for its very presence reached me at my essence level. Time and time again this deep sacred connection brought me into a unified space, and I felt reborn.

Black Elk began his teachings by taking me into a forest, and as the animals emerged, I would learn the symbolic meaning of their presence. I learned how to call in each animal for its ability to assist in healing. Humility was being taught by revealing the nature of the inner-connectedness of all life. The humble ways of Black Elk's people and their way of honoring all that is on this Earth were true messages of humility. I understood what was shown to me on a cosmic level, it simply made sense. And all the while, gratitude became an intensely deeper way of life. The glorious joy of learning so much, so fast, was many times overwhelming, and yet, I felt I couldn't learn fast enough. Knowledge of crystals and stones seemed to be learned so easily as their healing abilities were revealed to me. Because these teachings took place in that space beyond the rational mind, I was able to see that which cannot be seen with ordinary eyes. It was then I learned that at every given moment we have a choice, and each choice no matter how small, has a consequence as well as a power to create what can be in our lives. My heart had also been blown wide open, preparing me for a rigorous adventure. Through these sacred meditations with this Enlightened Being, awakenings from deep in my soul brought into my knowing the reverence for all life, and I was becoming one with that knowing. The cosmic love and connection felt for this loving guide was beyond anything ever experienced, or anything that could possibly be put into descriptive words. He had become my soul companion, but I did not know what that was at the time.

As the meditations progressed, Black Elk shared his vision with me. Through a series of meditations, he revealed this vision to me. In his vision, he was taken up to the Ancient Grandfathers and given the power to see the world through the eyes of the Divine. The gifts given to him from the Elders were the gifts activated from within his soul. He was told that these gifts were already there, he simply was given the extraordinary opportunity to awaken by experiencing direct communion with the Ancient Grandfathers. Through the eyes of his culture, he was able to see the peace and true harmony of all peoples and all sentient Beings as the one truth that transcends all cultures. It was both extraordinary, and yet ordinary. It being ordinary because when this type of transformation happens for someone, it doesn't mean they are "special." In a way, they are chosen for the experience because of their ability to handle that experience. But only to the mind would this qualify as specialness. The truth is the "knowing" that this is how some humans/souls are asked to receive teachings of the Divine. Sometimes there are no physical teachers on their journeys, and that is extraordinary.

It was not realized until 11 years later what actually took place at that time. I have recently learned that Black Elk's vision, which was shown to me energetically through the meditations, was meant as a symbolic map, as so many similar maps have been given in all cultures. This map showed the possibilities of how the world could be if we embraced the truths that were revealed to him. During many meditations he would tell me to "save his people." For years and years I never knew what that meant. And at that time, it was almost disturbing because the messages I would receive did not make sense to me. But there would always be comforting words and more gifts given. Each time a further plateau was reached in my consciousness, Black Elk would bring the message that *"You will now walk differently on this Earth,"* reassuring me that my perception had reached a higher way of "seeing." It's always almost humorous when we look back and see that sometimes we are not supposed to know, because we must experience a thousand or more "little" things to bring us to the one "knowing."

With recently receiving the Grace to come into a complete understanding with which his words were spoken to me all those years ago, I now have a crystal clear meaning. It was obviously not the literal command to go to the Native Americans. What I now understand from his words *"Save my people"* was the plea to "save" the conscious ones. In other words, helping those who are ready and willing to hear and understand truth, the true Nature of God and the true Nature of the Universe. By bringing the Mystical Universal Laws as the seed crystals, it thereby would start the transformation process needed for their world to evolve, so the world as we know it could authentically evolve. He understood that everything from within is also without. And in this understanding knew that this way of the world, and its potential for harmony, could only come from the sacred teachings of the soul. I have always felt deeply honored that the simple, humble and yet profound teaching brought from this Holy Soul made its way to me, so that I could bring my soul's purpose to light. It provided me with a renewed and deeper understanding of how to help others in the evolving of humanity.

All you Old Ones, Elders...
Who needed the buffalo for your survival
You knew of honoring what you had to take.
We now desperately need your help
To show us how to use only what is needed.
Please, with your wisdom of Old,
Guide us back to honoring.

As this deepening continued. In daily meditations, other Native American Beings brought gifts and guided journeys into my realm of healing. Another guide that was with Black Elk many times, was a Native American woman named Showanda. She was a continued source of the sweetest, most compassionate and loving mothering energy I can possibly describe. Everything about her was the Divine Mother's love. And I now, with so much gratitude and awe, realize that Showanda as my guide was the cosmic Holy Archetype of Mother Mary.

What I have learned recently is another piece of the puzzle that I've never known. It came as a revelation of what I experienced on May 21, 2003. I was meditating that morning with my friend. As Black Elk and Showanda were bringing me messages I began almost a type of hyperventilation. I found it difficult to get my breath while it felt as though I was going into a "shock state." This came out of nowhere, and while it was taking place I could feel something opening and being placed in me. It was a horrendous feeling, and my friend was trying not to panic. I became very cold and could not stop shaking for almost two hours. Black Elk asked me to be calm, and I could feel myself then recouping some oxygen. I was totally stunned and could not get up for a very long time. When I did my legs were literally like rubber, and I was so "foggy" I never knew what really happened. But I have the distinct memory of feeling "orphaned" for days afterwards, a feeling I've never experienced before. It felt like Black Elk and Showanda were my mother and father. At that time it was so strange because I hadn't felt that way towards my beloved "guides" before that intense morning.

The meaning of this was fully revealed nine years later when I learned that at some point in the mystical process of transcendence, sometimes one is opened up to receive the intense light of the Divine. This light is so powerful that one's physical body can't handle the vibrational frequency with which it is being brought into them. Our physical body, being the densest in our four body system, (physical, mental, emotional, and spiritual), will react in a state of shock or even as an epileptic seizure. I was very grateful to know what had happened all those years ago. I came to realize that the masculine/feminine guides were ultimately the sacred masculine/feminine forces being brought out from my soul. I learned that ultimately there is no separation of the masculine/feminine energies, as in the soul all is united as one unified power. This power is united as a passionate fire. Sometimes speaking the truth from one's soul requires this fiery force, and it also requires the gentle wisdom of the Divine feminine. As with Divine paradox, the feminine can also hold the fiery force, while the masculine may embody gentle compassion.

Both guides brought this sacred balance for a new wholeness to start within me.

And in recognizing all of this deeply, I knew that the feeling of being orphaned from a mother and father was the period I had to pass through, as I started to integrate what was taking place on the physical level, and was being incorporated into the deeper levels. The dramatic shift that occurred caused a shift in the consciousness of my soul. This brought the feeling of my guides as my mother and father. My soul had accessed the truth of Mother/Father God as the unified union. But on the more conscious levels I could not recognize it yet. The process of feeling orphaned is the natural phase until the light placed in us filters into all levels of our Being. Or, in other words, another plateau on the mountain has been reached and we must sit and let it become our Being. At that part of our evolving journey it is a "becoming process" of how to actually live it. As always, we can only "become" something through experiencing situations that allow us to "become" it.

My life came into a time of continually realizing and releasing old beliefs about myself and life, which allowed the openings for those healings to bring transformations. It was a time of illumination. Many times I was guided to access the precise book that held the message just given. This brought confirmation of what I was hearing and learning. I was grateful for such reassurance, because many times I was confused. I knew this way of learning was not usual, and sometimes found myself questioning what I was hearing. I didn't have enough spiritual knowledge at the time to realize that the challenging times came when my rational mind tried to "figure it out." There were also times when I took what was being said in a literal text, and not through the symbolic language from the soul. Several times I was asked to read the biblical story of Job, and did not understand why. I didn't know then that the tests of faith leading to his final surrender were the pathways into the transcendence of the mystical soul. And what certainly was not known was how this would be forthcoming into my life.

This process was taking place within to open my consciousness to higher levels, so that I could see how to clearly interpret what was being shown. Eventually, I began sensing how this process was actually changing my cellular structure and my DNA. There were many shifts on all levels that had taken place through my physical, mental, emotional and spiritual bodies. For me, there were physical changes as a result of the internal ones. Always having a sensitive system, my body intuitively let me know how to adjust my diet to handle even further sensitivities, as a permanent means of keeping my body open to the weightlessness of the light to come through. During this time, universal laws, the universal truths were continually being brought up from my soul and into my awareness. The animation of my soul was becoming my way of seeing the world. Everything on this Earth was different. It felt like I was in a whirlwind of learning. At times it seemed as though I couldn't learn fast enough. I was so hungry and so eager to absorb all that was being taught. This fire inside me burned so intensely and I knew with all my being that I had been called into the mystery of the Divine. Although at the time I could not language it that way.

As the deepening continued, the experiences of being suspended in a state of awe, where my soul was united and held in this space, also deepened. These raptures were ecstatic states of the mystery, where nothing here on Earth could ever come close to the totality of oneness experienced. There were different types of raptures, but each one held the same element. These holy connections to the Divine came spontaneously, in other words, very unannounced. Whether they occurred during meditation or when walking, these sacred invitations to the Divine always took me out of the senses and placed my soul into a holy and radically free space. Within a split second, my senses shut down, so to speak, as an intense knowing overcame every part of my being. Other times it was as if every fiber within was so intensely focused on absorbing what was happening in that brief micro-second that no part of my body could move. The one true element of each experience was the fact that I would only recognize that I had been shifted into a state of ecstasy after my senses had somewhat returned. It was only then that I was able to sit in a direct feeling of awe as I tried to have recollection of the experience. As anyone who has been blessed with such experiences knows, trying to put conceptual language onto this type of mystical state is not possible. But the knowing that you "now walk differently on this earth" is something that does not fade away.

At that time in the meditations, my love and connection to Christ had become an intense passion that paled everything else in my life. My soul was on fire with the eternal truth of every soul. I had been lit to serve the Divine, no matter what it took in my life to do so. It became the very breath I was breathing. I was blessed with the understanding of a powerful teaching from these experiences. The profound wisdom from Jesus to *"Be in the world, but not of the world,"* met my soul with the undaunted knowing of this truth. In my naivety, however, I didn't realize that by praying to be of passionate service, one must be totally purified. As many others know, once we fully surrender to God we are then required to become a clear channel. Our deep intention must evolve us past the limitations and illusions that still are hidden. I feel we are not forewarned about this part of the unfolding, possibly because if we knew how challenging it was going to be, we would choose fear and feel that we could not be able to endure it.

The deep sacredness that is the essence of these experiences continued to connect me, time and time again, into areas within. It drove me into deep prayer and self knowledge. I continually sought quiet places and the silence they held. My soul would speak of my highest potential, although I really did not understand at the time. I was asked to accomplish something that seemed so far fetched. It was also explained to me that I would write a book that transcended all religions, cultures and traditions. I had no idea then what that meant. Not yet knowing how to language what I learned, I didn't realize that *what* I was learning was transcendent of all traditions and religions.

Chapter 3

Illumination and the Dark Night

THE BLESSINGS OF MANY DIFFERENT experiences in meditation progressed. Some seemed bizarre at the time, until I realized that many worlds simultaneously exist at once, and we're all always part of that existence. The Angelic realm emerged in a powerful way through the daily meditations, and I realized that the magnitude of Grace which is continuously surrounding us is incomprehensible. We are able only to access a glimpse of this angelic power *because* of its magnitude.

The most profound gift from the Angelic realm happened one night as I slept. I was startled out of a sound sleep when our bedroom was filled with a huge illuminated "man". I sat straight up in bed and grabbed my husband's leg, telling him that there was a man in our bedroom. This illuminated Being was so large he filled every inch of space in the room with his light. He was walking towards me with the "Gift of

Eternal Life" in his hands. It looked like an ancient chalice type of vessel. I intuitively knew what it was, for deep within I recognized it as the true knowledge of the soul... the Divine Eternal Truth. I felt an incredible peace, while at the same time I was shaken from the experience. I was in a state of awe, gratitude, and almost a disbelief that it could happen to me. All of this played out in a micro-second. But the memory is still so vivid that even after ten years, as I think of it now, it feels as though I am seeing it play back as a movie.

My husband did not "see" this Being, as he thought I was talking about a regular physical human man. Because he did not recognize that it is possible to experience such a thing, that experience set in motion a chain of events. At this point I had no idea what was emerging from his inability to understand. Throughout this time I had been guided by teachers of different realms, and I had eagerly shared these meditations with my husband. Being in a state of awe with what was being learned, and how it was being learned, I naturally wanted to share it with the one I loved. I can still remember the excitement with which I replayed what was happening. I had entered that part of my soul that held understandings of the universe that somehow I already knew, and yet it was so exciting to re-learn it! I did not realize that he was pretending to agree with me. By nodding his head it appeared that he was understanding what I was saying.

As this journey continued, I found it extremely fulfilling when people began coming for spiritual tools and wisdom. I began working with those who came, and the more I helped others heal, the more I healed. Transmuting others' energy happened much more frequently. The energy of my Christ Consciousness had been accessed, and continued revelations with this pure and Enlightened Being became a mystical melding. There were many meditations with Jesus. These meditations for myself and others almost always took place by an ancient well, or on a beach by a body of water. There were different messages of how water symbolizes and is purification.

Some of the time Jesus would take my hand and we would go for humble walks. I could feel Him as a deeply compassionate friend and teacher. I cannot truly share how gloriously holy this was to experience. The pure humbleness of Jesus embodied me. I glimpsed both the most gentle and yet fiercely compassionate Grace all at once. The message of being imprinted with Christ's energy was brought, time and time again, in meditation. I had never heard of that before, and did not know what it meant, but I knew I was almost pulsating inside with His sacred teachings. Black Elk and Christ often were together in meditation, letting me know that this Divination process is available for all souls.

Upon reflecting, I am now able to present a view of how well choreographed this stage of our journey actually is. I can now see that we are given some form of amazing mystical glimpses, and even experiences, while some sense of our self is still intact. It seems as though this wonderful awakening is given to provide us with a taste, so to speak, of what will be waiting for us after we go through our real purification. Our soul would not have the strength to progress through the true purification fire if we were not given these glimpses, to use as the strength needed, as we have our remaining sense of self stripped away.

Situations were emerging through my family because of my passion to be of service. This purpose had become so strong in me that they could not understand why I was nothing like the person I used to be. As the universal truths continually emerged into my awareness from each revelation, it became increasingly more difficult to know how to proceed in daily life as everyone else was living it. Realizing this was for me a time of a bittersweet mixture of ecstasy and agony. I was so profoundly grateful for the experiences taking me deeper into the Divine. And yet, knowing what I knew, it was very painful to be with a family who could not acknowledge something different beyond their belief systems and five senses. It was an excruciating experience of not being able to reach them. My loving intent was to bring a glimpse of the freedom from their stress and into the passage of the true happiness that lay inside them.

I started to see how unwelcome any change is to the dynamics of family. Being the first to step out of the "family box," I became the focus of everyone's worry, which then led to resentment. As we change our interior life, our outer life naturally follows with changes. The need for quiet and solitude often is seen by others as depression. The releasing of old patterns and thought forms are naturally let go of by crying. When we experience this process, the ways of our "old self" are being shed. The more pain we bravely confront, the more intense the release is. For family and friends who have not awakened to their inward journey yet, this process can seem as an emotional imbalance and illness.

I have great compassion for those who recognize their inner need to grow away from the roles that families want them to abide by. Many thousands of us are being asked to be agents of change by bringing awareness of truth to our loved ones. I didn't know at that time this was what was being asked of me. I didn't know this was a calling from the Divine to provide a needed change in others' levels of consciousness. I just knew that my one passionate desire was to share what I knew, so they could also know. But many families will band together with an angry and degrading force aimed at trying to "break you down," because they do not wish to hear the truth you have discovered in yourself. It threatens the family unit as they know it, and the fear of change brings out dark reactions and painful actions. Humiliation, being another part of the mystic's path, becomes a very real factor at this time. As all of this became our reality, needless to say, it was extremely challenging. But in the challenging chaos was the Divine, who had perfectly orchestrated precisely what was needed for growth, for all involved.

The teachings I had been receiving and sharing with my husband were, unbeknownst to me, being relayed to three psychiatrists. My experiences were looked upon as emotional illness. A few of my children had entered into the field of medicine in their careers, and therefore, enforced their belief that drugs were the only way to change things back to "normal" with me. Because none of their consciousness levels had reached beyond the five senses, their eyes had not yet been opened to a possibility of evolving past the world as they knew it. After pleading with me to seek their way of help with medication, my family moved out. In trusting my husband with the sacred experiences of my journey, I was devastated when I learned of his actions of betrayal.

I did not know then that betrayal is a necessary part of the mystic's path. All I knew, at that time, was that I was taken down into the darkest point in my life. The betrayal came from those I truly loved, they were not the enemy. This caused a pain so great it was devastating. I began to experience the dark night of the soul. The dark night of the soul is the terrifying space where all that is familiar, loved and comforting is taken from you. Nothing is understood. When we enter this part of our path, we do not recognize it at all. We don't know that this well-planned period in our lives is to purify all within us that must be purified in order to fully enter into the authentic calling to God. No matter what path we are on when we enter into a chaotic and devastating time in our lives, it's always for a time of profound growth and change. Even though the true dark night might not be a process you are asked to undergo, the purification period is *always* designed perfectly for the evolving of the soul.

During the first phase of the dark night, it is precisely that – DARK. The darkness that surfaces within us from the betrayal, hurt and devastation, takes us deep into anger and blame. It brings up all which has also laid dormant inside from the past. The haunting and continued question as to why this is happening, and that it should not be happening, is predominant. We are so far down in our sorrows that we have no clue we are experiencing this for our learning. We only want the pain to end, and end quickly. It is a time when we feel so powerless, because all circumstances in our life seem to be unbendable. As the situation continues on, our "this is not fair" thoughts reach an all time high. Panic and blame become our temporary companions, as we are asked by the Divine to be pressurized into a melting pot that is so extreme we feel as though we can't bear anything else. A true dark night makes one feel as though it just can't get any worse, with no end in sight. Structure after structure must be stripped out of us, so that nothing of "us" remains as we knew ourselves to be. It simply must happen this way, because this is the direct path of Christ, and it's essential to come to know ourselves at the core.

Those who are truly dedicated to this path must experience in their own way, through their own life, the same type of experiences that Jesus as the man walked through, and then resurrected as The Cosmic Christ. This intense path requires us to experience our own "crucifixion," which is perfectly designed to crucify whatever our deepest fears are. It also means many times living through deep humiliation on multiple levels. When I was put into a physically humiliating situation by my children, even though I was confused and upset, I remember telling myself, with a direct knowing, that this was the crucifixion. And that deep knowing gave me strength, because I also knew that there would someday be a resurrection.

This dark night requires the strength beyond what we realize we actually have, a dedication in prayer, and an ongoing endurance. Even when we feel abandoned by God along with our friends and family, we must continue on, using prayer as the one foundation in which to make it through. I recall in that part of the process, I found that for me, nature brought an incredible and vast amount of healing. As a child, I would spend many afternoons in the woods near my house. That was where I felt truly at home and where the trees were my best friends. After the accident, I had spent more and more time out in all the seasons of nature. But it was when everything as I knew it in my life fell apart, that I truly reached into the woods... and spoke... and prayed... and asked... and received. I would return day after day because it grounded me and gave me a sacred place to grieve alone. The soul of the woods, all of nature was the comfort my heart needed then. The woods and animals held the symbolic learning that my soul so resonated with for healing the grief that was being released. The gratitude of being amongst the beauty offered by the woods always made tears of humbleness and gratefulness flow. There were many hours of just "being there" and actually feeling the healing taking place inside. Seeing the Divine in every leaf, stone, and of course every beautiful flower, helped nourish the crushed parts inside of me back to life.

For each of us that experience the dark night, the length of time we are asked to endure is varied. How long it takes us to be melted down to liquid by the intense fire of pain is up to each of us. It is in the "alone time" that we can find the resistance to what we are going through to be at an all time high. The fear of being alone is something that everyone holds somewhere inside. If we go deep enough, we can find it to be the most terrifying of realizations. If we really look with enough depth, we can see how neediness and grasping stem from this fear.

What we are not aware of is that the Divine must take us out of relationships and even our work areas, so that we can be taken deeper into the quiet to hear the Divine voice. We are given the opportunity to listen, instead of being overwhelmed by the noise of the world. Usually at that point we are not aware of this at all, because guarded deep inside us lies the fear that if we get closer to the Divine and further from the importance of the world, then we will always be alone, or at best, alone much longer that we care to be. Our awareness of these hidden fears, and what we choose to do with that awareness, helps determine how long this part of the dark night will continue.

As we are filled with emotions that rise up out of the dormant and hidden spaces within us, the natural release of tears seems to flow without end for a while. We start to wonder how one human can possibly have so many tears emerging. How do we get through the suffering? Eventually, somehow we have a knowing that we have to find a way to endure. Then, slowly, from somewhere deep inside, a glimmer, a Grace, comes into our consciousness. This glimmer is the realization that we can choose to love, more than we choose to continue to hold onto what we so dearly think we have to control. When this Grace becomes real in our lives as a way out of the deep pain, we realize that we must look at our illusions, our need for justice as *we* see it, and our way of holding judgment about the way things happened in our lives. And we begin to see that the descent into disillusionment is the way to receiving the transformation towards the Divine.

Eventually the kicking and screaming, the bargaining with the Divine, and the feelings of injustice subside to a point where we reach the second phase of the dark night. This is the crucial time when we start to realize that the end of our world has not happened and we will not only survive it, but can actually see for the first time, a softness enter into our lives. That "softness" we could call the beginning of surrender. It is when we feel we can take a deep breath and have a small degree of peace, of inner strength, that we didn't realize was there before. The dark emotions have started to turn into acceptance. We might start to realize that this whole thing was essential, it had to be for deep learning. This seems to be the point when we are called into real prayer. The irrational chaos of our lives has almost forced us to dive into our interior selves, because there is no other way to continue onward. True honesty and humility is essential for authentic prayer. We must look within with as much honesty as we can, to truly forgive ourselves and others. We can even start to realize some of the parts we held in ourselves as a way of staying angry.

We begin to pick up the pieces of our self, but in doing that we realize they aren't the same type of pieces they used to be. When we look at who is emerging from this fire that melted us into liquid form, we see that a different way of "seeing" has become our internal eyes. And our ears are hearing a compassionate inner voice that asks us to forgive. This process of healing is, more often than not, just as challenging as being in the fire. We must realize that when we make a choice to continually reach to the Divine for courage, the strength we need is always granted. As we pull from the illuminated experiences that took place before the dark night, we tap into the knowings from the place within the soul. Those experiences are a direct ally for strength.

As I experienced this process, prayer naturally entered my daily life with more of an intense dedication. I found myself praying like I had never prayed before. But I was not asking in prayer for myself. I had become an active channel of Grace. I began beaming that force known as Grace through me. It flooded to my husband, children, and all others who were associated with the situation. Many, many evenings were spent sending this Grace while asking for their forgiveness, and forgiving them. This all took place energetically. At that time, it took a great deal of strength on all levels, but I was continually blessed with strength, and very determined to reach a space of peace within me for all that had happened.

Throughout this process, I was realizing that I was being called to respond to my family in a higher manner, a sacred manner. The revelations from the Christ Self had taught, and were teaching me, to respond in a different type of love. This love was actually a willingness to take on their pain by not fighting back. It meant rising above a personal heart into a cosmic heart. It took a knowing that, no matter what was said or done, the ability to forgive, accept and honor was the only way to proceed. It took much perseverance and *practice*. When we make a conscious decision to truly surrender to the knowing that everything that has happened was perfectly placed for our learning from the Divine, our personal heart makes way for a more sacred way of loving. We then humbly learn how to reach in prayer for the Grace of Understanding, and not for anger, resentment or judgment.

With this Grace, we can seek to recognize the lessons that are available to learn from that chaotic period in our lives. For with this Grace of Understanding we know that the Divine is working in the chaos and we understand that it needs to happen… we get it! But the practice of rerouting our way of "seeing" takes a daily devotion. And it is definitely not easy at first. Therefore learning to forgive ourselves is also included in the way of this devotion. We are asked to heal the unloved part of ourselves. This core act of healing is the Mystic's way of sacredly walking on this Earth. Once we have experienced the energetics of true forgiveness from deep within us, we are able to receive extraordinary wisdom.

With this wisdom, we enter a new arena in our life. Our soul is going through a realigning process, as well as a strengthening one. Our soul is maturing. A deep joy is recognized, and we know it is emerging with a sense of permanency. It feels like a grounded part of us, because we know it is in our being, and we know it is coming *from* our being. This joy brings us into the transformation of knowing we will be okay no matter what. This is truly an inner joy of glorious and sacred spaces, enabling the Divine to shine forth from us. This opening, created by our intent to forgive, brings a deeper period of self-reflection. Slowly, more self-knowledge unfolds from the core of our soul. It can only be revealed in small increments, for we are tapping into spaces of great light, and we are also revealing the deepest fears still held within. It can be a time of imbalance, for as the light breaks through, giving us "new eyes" to live in truth, it can be increasingly difficult to quiet the mind from those fears held within. It is almost as if the mind strengthens its grip on the old thought forms and patterns. I so lovingly call it "the gripper," picturing a crab that has caught our big toe and will not let go. It takes a lot of practice at that point to stay in the knowing of what is the truth.

We've got to retreat to the place beyond the rational mind. This place can be seen as a beautiful "garden shed" where our spiritual tools are lined up on the walls. These tools of inner knowledge are always there for us to utilize as we need. When we truly realize that the mind cannot bring forgiveness, nor can it bring healing, we are using the first tool. We must realize that the mind continuously plays repetitive chatter. Its random and justifying thoughts always keep us from accessing the Grace of forgiveness, and anything else for our highest good. Only the soul holds this Grace. This tool is simply the deep understanding that the mind is a warehouse of information and facts, and that our soul must hold more authority in our lives than our minds. An effective way to incorporate this understanding deeper within is by providing a daily meditation devoted to practicing mindfulness, by quieting the mind. Picture yourself slipping down past the mind and travelling behind the heart to a bridge. Crossing this bridge will lead you into your soul. Mindfulness is a process of refining the activity as well as the quality of active thoughts in the mind. It takes practice, like all other skills.

But, when we come to realize this deeply, beyond the conceptual stage, it is easier to allow the thoughts that are always coming in, to simply flow out. The "gripper" then isn't able to stay attached to our big toe. We have to use this tool continuously for however long it takes in order to be free of the gripper. In other words a quiet mind, a more disciplined mind, freer of judgments and receptive chatter, will become our way of perceiving. As we persevere in this arena of our journey, we actually detach our consciousness from old attachments and the need to be attached to them. This spiritual alchemy transcends the rational mind… goes beyond reason, and allows us access to mystical wisdom. We are becoming a more and more intricately beautiful snowflake.

Chapter 4

Transformation and Spiritual Tools

Throughout the 2 ½ years that I was alone, as I continued to grow in devotion to the Divine, the process of purification intensified. It had been years of being shaped and reshaped, with my soul as my intimate guide and companion. Further truths, often deep and painful from the past, had been brought up for the freedom of healing to liberate me once and for all. Each day, seeing with higher eyes from the cosmic heart was my determined intent. There were so many challenges and then so many tests of my faith, will and strength. And through experiencing those tests, I found that with tremendous help and guidance from being purified, residing in my soul had become permanent "living quarters."

The mystical alchemy process had embodied everything, it transformed everything. The inner bliss and contentment was the harvest that emerged from the new growth after the interior fire. It is amazing to observe how our interior selves are so much like nature. The flourishment of the trees, flowers, and grasses are always much more abundant after fire destroys the land of its old growth patterns. So too is the joy and freedom that flowers the creative force flowing through us for growth, after being devastated by the internal fire. Organically, at this level, the new brings more abundance for each day, providing us with the strength and stamina to nourish others, just as all of nature also does.

I've also had the observation, that when picking black raspberries, the ones that are somewhat hidden from the direct sun, the ones quietly tucked beneath a leaf, are the berries that are the deepest of color and the juiciest of all. It is the same way, when we reside in the soul. It is the ordinary, the humble ones content to be out of the direct light, content to be no one "special," that are quietly ripened to their peak (wholeness). They experience the richness of light coming to ripen them in a much more profound way. Nature always reflects our interior. As we truly observe the many ways, the beauty can be beyond our comprehension. We feel the great joy of how the simplest of life forms can teach us the way into our simplest form of life.

> *"When you walk across the fields*
> *with your mind pure and holy*
> *then, from all the stones and*
> *all growing things, and all animals,*
> *the sparks of their soul come out*
> *and cling to you, and then*
> *they are purified and become*

a holy fire in you."
(Hasidic Saying)

As with nature, the cycle of a new beginning came to be as my husband and three youngest children returned home. This new beginning continually asked me to access the second tool in the beautiful "garden shed." The particular tool, this soul wisdom, was the knowing to not take anything being said or done personally – which is true detachment. Accessing this tool meant stepping back from the situation and viewing it as a movie, without any part of myself in it. As it was just a "situation," I found it neither good nor bad, it was just something happening around me. I learned from my soul, the place of complete love, that when something was directed at me, there is the ability to let it flow right through and not cause personal identity to become involved. Prayer aided me as a source of strength and endurance necessary for me, at this time in my life.

This tool was taken off the shelf many times for the first few years of our new beginning. Because my husband had not reached into his soul yet, his heart was doing the perceiving. And his heart was still hurt and unhealed. During this time I had to keep that tool front and center. By continually stepping back, this tool kept me residing in my soul. Deep prayers continued and messages were brought for a deeper meaning of self-empowerment. I was being asked to speak up for myself and bring my truth through once more.

I karmicly knew that the blind spots in his part of our relationship were to be opened up for healing awareness to come in. I was being asked to be of service by speaking the truth, as the blind spots emerged. And I was being asked to birth a more empowered place within myself, with the power that comes from truth and honesty. I was being asked to trust someone who had not yet owned his past actions. With direct intent, I started speaking up when the resentment was being presented, realizing that he had not yet been granted the Grace of understanding. With prayer, the cosmic heart continued to bring the essence of compassion to each situation. I found that every time the truth was spoken it became an act of illumination, inviting him to respond.

One of the truths brought for his awareness was another tool in the beautiful garden shed. This tool was the invitation to give up the need to know why things happen as they do. This tool, this Universal Law, says to let go of trying to find a reason for everything. Because we all are programmed to have to know "why," it becomes our main focus, and all that *is* important is missed. The ability to see the symbolic beauty behind a situation, or the ability to be in the moment observing the situation does not happen, because we are so frantically trying to find out why, or why not. We will notice that even the smallest thing has to have a reason for our mind to be okay with it. We need to use this tool constantly and consistently in order to see what illusions we create. Our mind creates the fear of the unknown, leading us to believe that if we can "figure it out" we will have some form of control over whatever it is we need to find a reason for – we will feel safer. The mind will tell us time and time again that we have to justify with a reason, feel safe with a reason, or prove something with a reason. The wisdom of knowing that we do not have to know why something has happened, or is happening, is indeed challenging to obtain.

The challenge comes in from not having a true and sacred knowing that trusts the Divine. It comes in from thinking **we** have the control, and that we will be able to keep it if we only know "why." This is a particularly difficult part of relationships. In order to **not** be vulnerable to our partners, the tactic often used is this particular type of control. The mind simply takes whatever is being talked about and runs with it, thereby not allowing any part to go deeper or communicate any true feelings. This avoidance is how so many were taught as children to "stay safe" in relationships. And this type of dishonesty is what always leads to role playing, causing spaces to become stagnant where growth can't flow in, bringing spontaneity or creativity. Communicating true feelings is essential for having a relationship based on truth and not lies, directness verses indirectness. Buddha knew this as he said: "*A lie is sweet in the beginning, but bitter in the end. Truth is bitter in the beginning, but sweet in the end.*"

The more I trusted the Divine to provide courage and the active will to trust completely, I saw a birth of a more powerful self evolving in me that started the next phase of my journey for further being of service. I felt as though another branch of the snowflake was forming. This branch had strengthened the entire snowflake while forming other intricate branches simultaneously.

Chapter 5

The Natural Mystical Shifts Miracles

THROUGHOUT THE NEXT FEW YEARS, I was blessed with being able to help more people who came for sessions to learn Universal Truths. I found that everyone comes for the same reason: to find peace within. Everyone, whether they know it or not, is searching for inner peace on some level. Some came not willing to realize that the peace they seek is inside themselves. Instead they were looking for a "quick fix," and when they found out otherwise, they didn't come back. Some stayed long enough to learn basic levels of how to bring more self-empowerment into their lives, but once the truth of what was really needed to become healthy came clear, they also left. Fear at that point in their lives was stronger than the strength of the soul. Understanding that this is perfectly designed for them can only bring compassion.

By progressing into the first stage of their spiritual journey, they awakened to the Divine Origin. But the fear of seeing deeper stopped them from seeking inner growth. As a result, the ego becomes stronger and stronger, and the Divine Origin with the knowledge from the soul starts to fade. This person who started to find a degree of inner peace now bounces in life, usually existing between not being happy and being "relatively" happy. The rational mind has talked them out of using the tools needed for growth. For now, they have given up the quest for true inner peace. It is too threatening to their life as they know it, and the fear of change is too strong.

In witnessing this time and time again, I see that these are the people who need to be prayed for everyday, filling them with Grace to be re-awakened with strength for a return to inner growth. I felt very honored to plant whatever seeds I could, knowing that when it is in perfect alignment for their learning, they will sprout and bring change. And then there are those who stayed… stayed for the tools, the inner discipline, and the truth. These few mystics now recognize that they have been called. The sweet song of their souls sang to them, prompting them to search for that song… the mystical path to provide the authentic way of writing "their music."

Miracles have entered into some of these mystics' sessions. One woman had been abandoned by her father at the age of six, never seeing him again. During the sacred space that was being held for her, she met her deceased father in our guided meditation, and chose to release and forgive him on the deepest soul level possible. The energetics of this act were so powerful that an energetic volcano became visible, as she released in a brief moment the deep, deep pain from fifty years ago. She instantly knew with all her being that at age fifty-six she was at last free of the intense burden. For her this was a true miracle, freeing her heart. She also knew this was the start of truly fulfilling her calling to the Divine. Since then, her father has come in meditation bringing her a soul level understanding of the cosmic truths that needed to be learned between them.

Mystics have a different relationship to time as others know it. For many people the word "miracle" holds a grandiose concept of something that only happened to the Saints in the days of old through the Church. Some do not realize that we are all capable of natural energetic shifts we like to call miracles. But there must be an inner knowing that they are possible. The inner knowing always comes from the soul, bringing us an authentic trust. When the transcendence level becomes one with our being, and our biological systems are aligned with this level, we are never caught in time because the soul resides in the timelessness. When we reside in the soul, the realm of miracles is in that timelessness, and is available for those who are aligned with it.

For the Mystic, our cosmic wiring is such that we do not simply **believe** that miracles can happen, we just **know** it. Questioning whether a miracle can take place or not, never even occurs when we have the knowing. Unfortunately, many people would love to know that miraculous happenings can be true, but the rational mind is too strong to allow their eyes to truly see. Some also hold these natural shifts as a concept, saying they believe they happen, but even when witnessing one, the mind keeps it from truly knowing.

Here is an example. On a beautiful evening in May, our beloved dog, Sadie, was enjoying one of her frequent rabbit chases. Being a border collie, she loves the chase, but never really catches the rabbit. Somehow in this particular pursuit, she slit open almost the whole underside of her body. During surgery they found that she was punctured as well. After five days of recovering we noticed that she had worsened and the ultra thin skin has peeled away in some parts. Re-stitching was not an option, and recovery looked to be a longer process that what we had thought. I had told four other people of her injury and they were praying with all the angels for her. It was at this point after seeing her worsen, that I particularly asked Archangel Raphael for a spontaneous healing. Periodically, throughout the day I reached out in prayer. Early that evening my husband and I decided to walk down our lane to trim some grass. Sadie had still been unable to hardly walk at all, but much to our shock, she jumped up and was ready to come with us. Not only was she running up and down the lane, she also was playing catch with her toys, and playing with our cat. As I stood and witnessed this, my hand on my chest, I knew within that Archangel Raphael had responded to our prayers. It has been days since that evening on the lane and she has only continued to be her energetic fun-loving self.

The interesting part of this story, I feel, is in the response from the four other people who were praying for her. The first two people I told responded with a knowing and awareness that this was indeed a beautiful miracle. It was recognized as an amazing, but also possible, reality that does take place. The third person's response was one of "Wow, that's interesting," and the last person when questioned said he felt that the healing from Raphael *could* have played a part in it, but felt it wasn't all of the factoring of why she suddenly recovered.

These differing responses bring into full view the realization that when we are plugged into the knowing, what we truly ask for in prayer can be answered in the blink of an eye. Because we are plugged into the level of that knowing, we potentially have the ability to energetically pull the situation from the Universe that is necessary. When we do not know this is possible through higher consciousness levels, then miracles can never occur for us. The limiting viewpoint, the restricting belief, severs the link that would connect us to that reality. It does not allow access to the higher energies available. For some people, unfortunately, even witnessing such events as described above with Sadie, still does not break through the old belief system to give way for something more

Chapter 6

Another Soul Expansion
into Teresa of Avila

As THE MONTHS FLOWED BY, I continued to see people for sessions and also ran the expanded antique shop. Daily listening to my guidance provided direct and precise ways in which to council and heal others, and also continued to drive me deeper into myself. I realized that the energetic work on people's chakras and grid systems was a skill from my soul - through my soul, and that it was becoming more laser-like and more powerful. Remembering that humility and gratitude must always be front and center to remain as an open conduit through which the light can flow through, was a daily dedication which I took very seriously.

Mystical experiences continued to happen, out of nowhere there would be messages brought, or I would be mystically overtaken with a Grace of the pure beauty of something. When my Mom died early in March 2010, my husband and

I flew to Arizona for the funeral. We had a brief time to walk in the mountains, and as we walked, I suddenly could not move. I stood looking out to the sky from a flat part in the mountain and literally gasped as I inwardly felt myself expand once again. It was an expansion so vast, so deep, and I realized in that split second I was one with the vastness of the mountain and all of the Universe. It's as if the power of this vastness in the mountains reached inside me as I reached for it simultaneously. It overtook me and the tears choked me as I tried to get my bearings to continue walking on. It was an absolutely beautiful, deeply joyous and sacred moment. I recognized a deeper vastness of the soul as never before.

Upon waking the next day after returning home, I knew with all my being that I was to build a "healing home." I was to call it Essence Healing Home, and was precisely guided to take one of the antique buildings, empty out all the contents, and build it into something totally new. I knew it would cost thousands of dollars to accomplish this, but I also knew the certainty with which this guidance came. I trusted it would emerge precisely as it should. The next day I gathered those who were able to put in hours to make it happen. Everything went very smoothly and within three weeks or so, Essence Healing Home had a separate half of the building on the left for sessions. The other side was still available for customers to shop. It had become a tea room and book store, with many books for sale and treasures from nature to warm the soul.

For a year this worked well until it was understood that I was to expand even further. It was then I knew I had to use the entire building as the healing home. Once this was accomplished, the energy throughout became very obvious to everyone who came in. This humble metal building had become an energetic "retreat," as people were continuously saying this was what it felt like for them.

It was then that I was blessed with learning an expanded way of teaching. So much came to me so fast. Hours and hours of absorbing new ways of languaging what I already was teaching were extremely exciting. It was a richly encompassing means of presenting truth. I felt as though my soul had been just waiting for that perfect timing to acquire expanded avenues that would help others to also expand. During this time I learned of the work of Teresa of Avila. As I read her book, "The Interior Castle," describing the seven castles which are the consciousness levels of the soul, I realized with awe and gratitude that this was the process my soul had progressed through. Each castle held the truths I had learned through the experiences over the past eleven years. When I discovered her work, I felt as though all of me was lit from inside out, for she put into words what I knew.

As I started presenting the castles to those who came for sessions, I sensed an incredible closeness to Teresa. I felt her with us when we were in session. I found that I kept her book with me as much as possible, opening it whenever I got extra moments during the day. Before learning of her work, "The Interior Castle," I did not know who Teresa was. Now she was ever present in my thoughts, and at times I would sense her energy. I have so much admiration for her determined passion to bring truth from the soul. The endurance she acquired to **bring** those truths, led her to become the brilliant Mystic she was. And she is still assisting us by bringing the truths in our time of need.

On one particular Wednesday in late November I received a message to go up to the table and chairs in my bedroom. The sun was starting to set, and as I sat facing the reddish glow, I slipped into a meditative state and yet was still aware of watching the colors the sun was giving us in that moment. I then very loudly and precisely heard the words "Look and find me, I am here." I looked around the room, while at the same time knowing the voice was coming from directly across the table. I instantly knew by the presence of her energy that it was Teresa of Avila. She told me many things, but what I definitely remember was the part about writing the book that had been brought to my attention almost nine years before. Her words and energy were very precise, but gentle. She relayed to me that I must write this book, and it was understood that she would be assisting me.

As I was with this Holy Being, I had entered into a state of mystical awe as she revealed in a brief timeless moment an amazing truth. With all mystical experiences that take us into this sacred realm, finding a way to language it is almost impossible. To the best of my ability I would be able to say this... in that moment of deep revelation, I was able to see with utter clarity all that had played out in my journey from the past eleven years. It was as if this revelation contained the secrets from the Divine, as a confirmation of what I deeply knew through the years, but had not *fully* incorporated. It was a true confirmation of all the events that took place. In that Divine moment, for example, I understood deeply the importance and symbolism of Black Elk in my journey. And as everything played in front of me, as I caught my breath, I realized I had traveled the true path of the Mystic. Without even knowing of The Castles, the evolution with my soul had propelled me through each of them. This confirmation stunned me, embraced me, and saturated me all at once. All was known at a deeper depth within me.

As I sat taking all this in, my husband came home from work unusually early. All of my senses were not fully engaged as the awe was still lingering in me. He instantly saw that something had taken place, and I could only be very open and honest with him, and share what had just transpired. I intuitively knew that his unexpected arrival home was Divinely orchestrated, so that there would be an opening for us to look at parts in my journey that were never addressed or understood after they had happened. I spoke for hours, and while relaying with tears from the sacredness of what I had experienced, I believe there was an understanding in him that he had not had before. I felt he realized what occurs while evolving on the Mystic's path, although he was not able to directly speak it.

After this encounter with Teresa, everything felt different in my life. It seemed as though I had been birthed into a truth that was not fully comprehended before. There was a marvelous completion like I'd never ever known – a radiant wholeness of being. With this deep recognition of my path as a Mystic, I then saw clearly – exquisitely clear – that the process of evolving Essence Healing Home for the past few years was for the purpose of creating a "Monastery" for those few Mystics who were regularly coming for sessions. It had become a type of sanctuary and a tranquil haven to retreat into providing the sacred space necessary while inner releasing is being done. The people who came for sessions knew that the door was always open, and having a safe loving space to learn mystical laws enabled them to unfold into who they truly are. They recognized it as a spiritual Monastery. I felt so totally blessed and my heart flooded with great joy as I really realized the true meaning of why this farm evolved as it did.

I knew then that Teresa had been with me long before I sensed her presence. She had continually guided me to create the type of monastery that is so necessary for all those who are realizing their true paths now. I learned through her how to build, with the sacredness of the soul, a place for Mystics in search of Truth. It had to be built with authentic trust, without agendas or expectations. The soul work through the castles enabled this to be a reality on Earth. Knowing that this is how I am to be of service, right now for others, brings the deepest, depth of honor and joy into me as I so passionately aim to give it back out. I am filled to the brim with sacred happiness, and I have realized that the branches of my snowflake have formed extended intricate patterns from the Grace of the Divine held together with wonderment.

Chapter 7

A Noble Suffering

W E NEVER KNOW WHAT THE Divine will ask any of us. I feel that this is what makes the journey in each of our lives so intriguing. About three weeks after my encounter with Teresa, I was bed ridden with pneumonia. It came out of nowhere with a fever of 103.5. I immediately knew with all my being that I was being asked to undergo another cocooning phase. I also knew I was being asked to undergo a noble suffering. It was a noble suffering in that I knew it had a purpose, and also knew it would mean suffering on the physical level. In surrendering to that was the wisdom of also knowing the Divine would be teaching me so much. Being asked to undergo a noble suffering is quite an honor if we choose to see it that way. It means taking off your watch as to how long it will last, and using prayer not to escape the suffering, but to deepen yourself within it. Authentically trusting that it has a purpose, and knowing that pain always precedes a birth, allows an endurance as well as an excitement of what the birth will bring.

During the two days when the fever stayed at 103.5, I would be in and out of consciousness. As I came in, I would have a strong lingering remembrance of being in a very old Monastery with Teresa. I could barely recall the feel and smell of it, like a faded memory, but it would come back with me each time. It is difficult to describe the feeling of it. It was almost eerie, and yet so wonderful, all at the same time, like a secret holy fullness within me. Within six days of having pneumonia I then contracted a viral infection that took me down. The physical suffering was one I had never known – (not ever being sick except for the flu a few times). As I lay in bed for days, I was given an opportunity to pray. I learned to pray for others from a humbler place, for I had been stripped down to a very humble place in my daily life. With the strength I did have I used to read Teresa's work. I found that the soul work with her was almost constant, and I felt so blessed for this time.

On a crisp winter Sunday morning as I lay in bed, I started talking to my husband about a few mystical raptures that had taken place since I had been sick. For some unknown reason, I asked him if he remembered when we had seen that unusual butterfly at the forest preserve two summers before, and how upon gazing at it, I was overtaken by her beauty. I was taken into another realm where I actually felt "drunk" on the exquisite Grace of this particular butterfly. I then commented to him that I felt like I was coming out of this cocoon time as the butterfly. About half an hour later, my son saw something in one of the trees in our back yard. As he ran out in the snow and cold to get it, I couldn't help but giggle and feel the joy as he brought in a beautiful balloon in the shape of a butterfly! None of us could figure how it could have landed perfectly in one of our trees. Especially having no holes after landing in the country in winter. It made me smile as I felt a reply from heaven coming in the form of a helium balloon. What an awesome sense of humor heaven has!

Chapter 8

Heavens Gentle Nudge

ANOTHER REPLY FROM HEAVEN ARRIVED in a bit more serious package about a month later. While driving, my van's fuel pump broke, leaving me absolutely no warning, I had to pull over to the side of the road. This was a bit serious because the back end of my extended van was on the highway at the top of a bridge in the blowing snow. As soon as it happened, I knew the definite message that was being brought in. There was no fear as I waited an hour for a rescue ride home. I knew that I was to start writing this book that morning instead of going to do errands.

Once back home, trying to get warm, I aimlessly walked around the house asking to be open for any clarity coming through. For the past few weeks, I had not known how to start this book, and I knew there was a part of me inside that was putting it off. As I was guided to look at the snowflake book that I keep on the coffee table in the winter months, it was then that the message to study the pictures of the snowflakes became loud and clear. Within minutes, the introduction poured out onto the paper. I felt very excited, relieved and blessed all at once.

It is now six months later and the last part of the book was brought through a knowing revealed last week. There are seven "properties" of the soul that Teresa has relayed as being important for one's radiant wholeness of being, and for sacred happiness to be an intricate piece of our daily lives. When we truly incorporate these and work towards obtaining them as our way of being in this world, then we are truly functioning at the highest level of human existence, thus bringing the Divinized Human into full empowerment.

These attributes are not new words or concepts, by any means. We have all heard these words before and are familiar with what they mean. By presenting them through the wisdom of the soul, they can be realized on deeper levels, bringing in their true meaning, and thus fulfill the expansion of our snowflake branches having woven in a richer and more intricate way to view our lives.

Chapter 9

First Attribute: Sacred Ownership

Ownership seems to be an attribute that is developed relatively early in the maturing soul for many people. Ownership is activated when we realize our part that took place in something that happened - when we see how irresponsible we were. It is when we recognize these parts of us that acted out of unhealthiness, and we then actively choose to acknowledge it by taking the responsibility needed to own it, either in prayer to the Divine or to the person who needs to hear our words.

Sacred Ownership goes beyond the simple "I'm sorry." It continues to go deeper as we claim our part, because we have stepped back from the situation to view it as a learning circumstance. And we then realize that "I'm sorry" does not extend enough healing grace to the other person or situation. When we cosmically own it in prayer, it becomes healed energetically and our karmic scale becomes increasingly balanced. What is equally important is the owning of our **own** dark spots, of **why** we acted out of unhealthiness. It's here where the process of the maturing soul becomes more challenging, because we must dig deep to see the core. The more chances that we take ownership of, as it comes up for us to own what we have done, or what are still doing, the freer we become through the energetics on all levels.

This attribute of the soul grows stronger as we mature into being able to own what we need to with more ease and determination. And as the soul comes into full maturity, immediate ownership becomes a type of disciplined "law" that is always upheld. If something needs to be owned, it is. It becomes our radical sense of responsibility for ourselves and all others. We are able to view ownership as a healed grace brought to whomever is involved, knowing that it also effects every other soul in humanity. As we are all connected to all energy, it can bring a blissful peace within, as we realize that our contribution of Sacred Ownership brought light into the universal flow of life.

Chapter 10

Second Attribute: Authentic Trust

A UTHENTIC TRUST COULD BE LIKENED to what we know as faith, and yet it can reside even deeper than faith. It unfolds in us from deep within. It is the attribute found as we uncover the knowing that all is perfectly designed for our learning, which then unfolds into the knowing that we will be fine no matter what happens. This Authentic Trust in the Divine comes from the sacred part in us that completely trusts *ourselves*. Totally trusting ourselves is a process in which we go through situations to "test" how much we actually do know and trust ourselves. We have all been through hundreds, if not thousands, of these "tests" as we continue to grow deeper in the process of self-knowledge and *trusting* that self-knowledge.

We can recognize when we are reaching Authentic Trust, for example when we have made a decision and we did not look to **question** our decision. Or as another example, when we leave our pet or even our child with someone, we say we trust, for the day. It is when we do *not* spend time worrying, wondering or questioning if they are okay. We simply trust that everything will be taken care of as it should be, by the person, and even more importantly, by the Divine. If we are still questioning, meditation will call us within ourselves to look at why. What fear can't I release to become one with *truly* trusting others, myself, and the Divine?

Authentic Trust is one of the most radically freeing attributes of the soul. It places us in a freedom that contains the sparkling essence of pure Divine bliss, because we continuously reside in the sacred knowing that "I will be okay no matter what," we then understand at the core level that the Divine alone provides everything.

Chapter 11

Third Attribute: Sacred Integrity

W HEN WE REACH THE LEVEL of Sacred Integrity, we truly learn who we are. We have come to understand on a deep level our areas of darkness and also our strengths from the truth of our souls. We have to pass through many levels of integrity before we transcend into the sacred realm of this attribute. Integrity begins with thoughts and acts that have become congruent. Such as keeping your word, keeping a secret when asked to, and knowing how to do the right thing when your conscience tells you to do so.

We then pass into a level of integrity that prompts us to speak up for ourselves, and stand our ground when being questioned. And as we come into Sacred Integrity, we form such a strong bond to this sacred part of our soul that there are absolutely no separations. There is no personality residue that can sway us from this unity of sacredness. Our "personality," for lack of a better word, has been built out of steel, a grace filled sacred steel that only allows for this attribute from the soul to be our guiding force in every area of our life. As with all other properties, a process must be progressed through in order to access this part of us. We will be challenged in all areas of our lives until the essentially deep us becomes the undaunting force with which the Divine is the radiant core.

Chapter 12

Fourth Attribute: Honoring

O N ANY SPIRITUAL PATH, HONORING is extremely essential. We learn from being guided by our soul how to honor nature, other humans and all sentient beings. In a maturing soul, the next step in honoring is honoring ourselves. We start by learning how to take better care of our bodies through exercise, healthy eating, etc. Then we start to realize that we need to *really* honor our bodies. In recognizing how important each organ and limb and cell is to our functioning bodies, we begin to have an aware appreciation for each part. Thanking all parts of our body for their service to us each day becomes very important as our way of honoring the body.

The process then takes us into an awareness of how to truly honor others with less judgment, expectations and agendas. A new sense of respect emerges with this honoring, as we recognize how different we all are and yet how we are all ultimately the same. Then as the soul reaches higher levels of consciousness, we are aware that we are asked to honor the Divine with those higher levels. We strive to know the Divine through a deeper level of prayer. We learn that honoring God is to be purely humble at all times in prayer, and that this humility must extend out to everything we do in our daily lives in order to truly honor in that manner from the depth of our soul. It is then we experience what Sacred Honoring is.

Chapter 13

Fifth Attribute: Endurance

ENDURANCE IS THE ATTRIBUTE THAT almost all people do not wish to know about. No one desires to go through something challenging for *any* length of time. Therefore, endurance is not recognized as a Grace given from the soul. It's only when we can realize it *is* Grace that we then know what we are going through, which lasts so long, is because we are being asked to learn endurance. It may be an illness, divorce or anything that requires an ongoing amount of strength, stamina and patience. As more and more people have moved into the "instant gratification" world, even the *word* endurance is not known.

Whether it comes to being physically uncomfortable or emotionally uncomfortable, pharmaceutical drugs are immediately reached for to "fix" the hurt. However, as our soul matures, we see that experiencing challenges for growth are absolutely necessary, and enduring them are also absolutely necessary. We can learn to look at an illness, or the difficult period in our lives, as being the time when we are asked to learn this invaluable attribute. By moving time and time again through each challenge in a steadfast and determined manner, in other words, persevering through the tough times with eyes wide open to see the truth of why it is lasting as it is, we are brought into the Grace-filled wisdom of Endurance. And we are held in a space of sacred deep peace as we have come to truly know that we can endure anything *with* the Divine and *for* the Divine. *"All good lies in perseverance,"* wrote Teresa of Avila. This is the enduring perseverance to become even closer to God. Endurance.

Chapter 14

Sixth Attribute: Sacred Gratitude

GRATITUDE IS PERHAPS THE MOST easily recognized attribute of the soul. We all have been grateful many, many times in our lives. We say thank you prayers for our meals, especially at the holidays. We give thanks when something goes smoothly during our day, or when we get what we "asked" for. This type of gratitude is only the beginning of gratitude. While it is necessary and worthy, Sacred Gratitude is the essential attribute for the soul to transcend fully to the Divine.

While we are indeed grateful for all that is given and placed in our lives that make it enjoyable, Sacred Gratitude enters in when we truly have the understanding to also be grateful for all that was so terribly difficult and challenging. This step that we take into understanding and fully knowing that everything had to be as it was, is the direct step into Sacred Gratitude, therefore we can be so grateful it happened the way it did.

Once we experience the depth of this, it never leaves us. It has been woven into our fabric of existence and without even realizing it, we continuously give thanks on an inner level for *everything*. It is not that we consciously "say" thank you for everything, it comes from that deep understanding and is a certain type of Grace that is continuously emanated by our thoughts. It's then that we can authentically be grateful for the sunny, bright days as well as the stormy dark ones. They all have their purpose and we are grateful that they do.

Chapter 15

Seventh Attribute: Sacred Balance

I T IS VITALLY IMPORTANT THAT we ask the Divine for Sacred Balance in all areas of our lives... balance of our inner and outer (Heaven and Earth), balance of our mind and heart, balance of our soul and body, and also balance of the masculine and feminine within us. This full alignment is so critically important when being of service in whatever way we are asked to be helping others. It seems as though the question Mystics have who are awakening to their calling – those who are realizing the old self and are working to rebirth into the new – is "How can I be of service?" I feel this is where Sacred Balance must come in.

So many have the idea that because their calling is one to the Divine, they need to accomplish big things, such as being famous, or starting businesses. There are many who truly feel that *only* by taking action to help save whatever they feel strongly about is the way they are to be of service. It is important to realize that taking action is indeed a necessary part, but the simple and humble act of prayer is also very necessary when being of service. To bring Sacred Balance into our knowing of how to be of service through each day, we must be especially aware of the *mind-body* interaction. The mind will, of course, tell the body to actively move to be of service and the body will respond. That being an important part, the Sacred Balance comes when we *also* have the quiet mind with the quiet body in times of deep prayer for all we wish to be of service to.

The Sacred Balance of the *soul and body* is living in the knowing that the Divine places us in the perfect place with the perfect timing for us to best be of service. This deep knowing comes from the soul, and when we abide in that Sacred Soul Balance, all unfolds with humility, naturally also balancing the *mind and heart*. The heart is always open to allow the question of "How" to be answered through the Divine's way, thereby bringing Heaven to Earth. A wise person once said that we should keep two pieces of paper in our pocket at all times. One says "I am nothing but a grain of sand," and the other says "The Universe was created for me." Balance: knowing that the power lies within and yet always keeping humility just as powerful. This is the mystical wisdom for our journey to being complete. This completeness is a soul that is equipped with perceptual skills, a mind that is sharp with common sense, and in between is a compassionate heart that has learned the ability to discern.

When truly experiencing the depth of the moment, in Sacred Balance, there is an awareness of the physical body standing present and also the sacredness being felt is almost touchable. And you realize that you are feeling the movement of the Universal Energy, and you *are* that movement, and with that depth you can feel what is actually coming to you on the physical level. Because the knowing is so deeply rooted, so deeply imbued with the Grace of the Divine, our spark within is in intense peace and joy that illuminates every cell within us, and provides an illuminated light around us. When we reside there during our daily activities, it's almost as if we walk so lightly that every step and movement we make is filled with Grace. This angelic feeling, as we could call it, is true communion with the Source – the Sacred Balance of physically taking part in daily activities on the Earth plane while retaining the higher consciousness of the "Heavenly realms" – all being One united in the Sacred Balance.

These seven attributes are like glistening gems within *each* of us. It is our job as souls on our journey making our way to the Source, to be as mindful as we possibly can to bring the sacred back into our world today. It has long been gone from people's lives, as it is obvious to see when looking at the state of humanity right now. In doing the best we can to be aware of the *depth* of these attributes, we can bring an authentic change to all sentient beings at this critical time.

Chapter 16

Wisdom of the Crystals

I N ORDER TO MORE EFFICIENTLY expand our snowflake branches, healing with a variety of methods is sometimes beneficial. As we know, crystals and gemstones have been residing deep within the Earth for millions of years. They too vibrate with a consciousness frequency as does every living and non-living thing in the Universe. Because they reside in a stillness that is beyond human comprehension, they contain the most sacred and highly vibrational energies found. As they lie so deeply encapsulated within the inner surface of the Earth, they remain still throughout each moment as they continuously absorb that precious energy while growing. Profound quiet is their constant home.

When we are fortunate enough to hold a crystal, we can feel the pure energy pulsing from it, allowing us to receive its sacred imprinted knowledge of stillness. As we connect with the crystal, it transfers this deeply rooted wisdom, bringing change to what is needed to be healed within us. By bringing its natural stillness into our energy field, it balances us by raising *our* vibrational energy. Crystals bring subtle shifts to the precise area that needs transforming. We only need to be open to receive this type of energetic healing. By placing these incredible healers in your home, or keeping them close to you, you enable the purest form of healing that the physical Earth has to offer. They are such a beautiful tool in aiding us energetically to become more elevated.

Chapter 17

Furry Soul Gifts

THROUGHOUT EVERYONE'S LIFE MANY GIFTS are received. One gift for me has been so powerful that I feel it needs to be shared. I call them "soul gifts" because it is so obvious to see the evolution brought by their presence. They are our two border collies. Sadie, a rescue, came to us first and through situations brought about by her, caused a glorious shift in the dynamics of our marriage relationship, bringing much growth. Shifra was five months old when she arrived unexpectedly in a truck here on the farm. She literally walked up to me and I heard her say "I'm here." Her soul is so pure, she knows only joy, and her sweetness absolutely melts us. I am so deeply connected to her that there have been times when I awake in the middle of the night from "seeing" her so vividly in front of me with a glow around her. And all the while she is sleeping in her bed on the floor.

As other pet owners also know, these creatures hold such sacredness. They live in joy that is seen by those who wish to see that they are continually blessing all of us who are with them. The tragedy of not being able to recognize this lies within those too ridden with pain to allow themselves any sight beyond their own inner turmoil. Through the blindness of their pain, often times their animals pay the price. We must pray for these humans to be filled with Grace as *much* as we pray for the animals who are being neglected and mistreated. As channels of Grace, this act of sending out Grace to those in pain who are *causing* creatures (and others) pain is using the Mystic's power with mystical wisdom to dissolve darkness. This sometimes challenging prayer has the ability to bring the physical action of rescue into a *deeper action of rescue*. It is the rescue of the soul. We must help rescue the souls of the humans who are damaging the souls and bodies of our beloved creatures. As many of us now realize, the critical time of prayer and of utilizing our spiritual tools has never been more important, has never been as critical for our survival. We are being called to work in bringing the formation of our individual snowflake into the intricate pattern of wonderment filled with the Divine.

Celestial Beings

In the inconceivable vastness in which we are all an intricate part, an analogy of celestial beings can be found.

The clouds symbolize form that is taken each time we return for a life journey here. Some are heavy and stormy, some are white and wispy, and some are solid and stable - all different depending on the lessons needed to be learned with each lifetime – always appearing and reappearing, mingled together, floating in the vastness.

We can see the sun as representing our being, our true essence that continually pours its warmth – our pure radiant energy - giving out to all. The days we experience overcast conditions are the times when the ego has covered up that golden stream of light. The atmosphere is filled with turbulence.

When kind acts take place, when respect for others and nature flow from us, we experience the sunny delightful days. When awareness and true compassion are being manifested, we revel in the absolute glory of a spring day bursting with sun-filled rays opening each flower, or stand and look in awe as the fall colors on each leaf are being touched by a ray of sunlight.

The moon embodies all of our cycles, in and out of form. Not only representing the change in nature's seasons, the changing of our life's phases, but also the next profound cycle of birth and death. Through this receptive balancing of cycles, we flow fluidly in the Universal Stream.

The stars could be thought of as our eternal self that is seen though all darkness, always present, but exceptionally beautiful when observed in the darkness that surrounds them. The biggest, brightest and most awesome stars can be viewed as the great way showers that brought the knowledge of the Universe in their time.

Their light is still shining brightly on us today.

About the Author

Josie Hopkin's life has been that of the Mystic. Her calling to this life began at age six, when after being revived from the dead she started the journey into the depths of her soul. The isolation and purification that is so necessary for this path was the way of life that lead her to reach the true understanding of mystical laws and universal laws. Residing in the deepest dimensions of her soul, the core essence, Josie has become a conduit for radiant wisdom, always allowing the divine to speak through her. Josie has been helping others on their spiritual path for over a decade. She yearns to witness and assist many more souls in awakening them to their calling.

"My heart's desire is to assist those who are willing to move past fear and illusion into their true core essence.
My life's purpose is to awaken the soul's wisdom and help connect you to the Divine light of all that is."
Josie Hopkins

Josie offers individual healing sessions and classes on spiritual development at her rural Essence Healing Home in Maple Park, Illinois

Website: www.essencehealinghome.com

CPSIA information can be obtained at www.ICGtesting.com
Printed in the USA
LVOW130041051212

309922LV00001B/1/P